POP CULTURE BIOS

NICHOLAS

HOULT

BEAST OF THE SILVER SCREEN

NADIA HIGGINS

Lerner Publications Company

MINNEAPOLIS

Lerner Publications Company
A division of Lerner Publishing Group, Inc.
241 First Avenue North
Minneapolis, MN 55401 USA

For reading levels and more information, look up this title at
www.lernerbooks.com.

Library of Congress Cataloging-in-Publication Data

Higgins, Nadia.
    Nicholas Hoult : beast of the silver screen / by Nadia
Higgins.
        pages   cm. — (Pop culture bios)
    Includes index.
    ISBN 978-1-4677-1444-0 (lib. bdg. : alk. paper)
    ISBN 978-1-4677-2502-6 (eBook)
    1. Hoult, Nicholas, 1989- —Juvenile literature. 2. Actors—
Great Britain—Biography—Juvenile literature. I. Title.
PN2598.H68H55 2014
791.4302′8092—dc23   2013021103

Manufactured in the United States of America
1 – PC – 12/31/13

INTRODUCTION

Nicholas greets his fans at a 2013 Hollywood event.

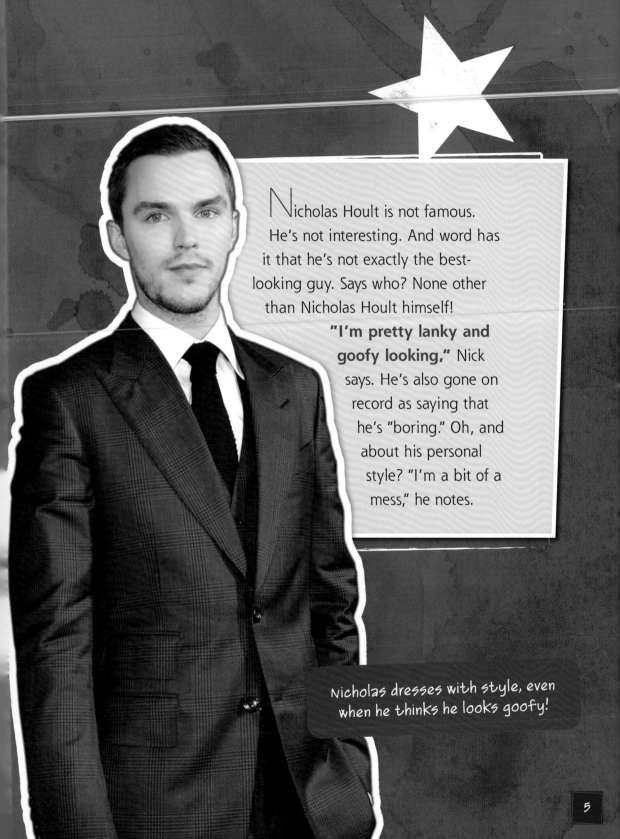

Nicholas Hoult is not famous. He's not interesting. And word has it that he's not exactly the best-looking guy. Says who? None other than Nicholas Hoult himself! **"I'm pretty lanky and goofy looking,"** Nick says. He's also gone on record as saying that he's "boring." Oh, and about his personal style? "I'm a bit of a mess," he notes.

Nicholas dresses with style, even when he thinks he looks goofy!

The British actor says all of this and more, even as he embarks on a huge press junket. It's early 2013, and Nick has the lead role in a major Hollywood movie. Actually, make that *two* movies! He stars as a lovable zombie in *Warm Bodies*, out in February. The next month, he's the unlikely hero in *Jack the Giant Slayer*.

Everyone else is saying that Nick is entering an exciting new stage in his career. So … is he?

"I don't know. Maybe," says Nick.

Is it the spell of those oh-so-blue eyes? That sly half-smile? That funny low chuckle? Maybe it's his habit of saying "blimey!" in the middle of interviews. One thing's for sure: no matter what Nick says, his fans are smitten!

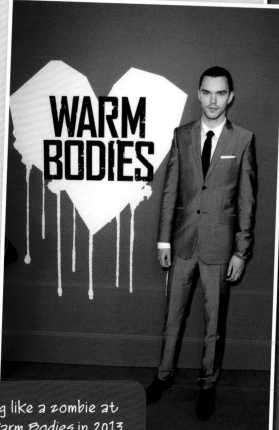

Nicholas looks nothing like a zombie at the L.A. premiere of *Warm Bodies* in 2013.

It's not that Nicholas has low self-esteem. It's not fake modesty either. He just really seems to like being the butt of his own dry humor. Still, there's one line he doesn't cross. Nicholas never says he's a bad actor. In fact, he lights up when he talks about acting. **"It's like playing,"** he (almost) gushes. **"Every day is different."**

So maybe it doesn't matter if Nicholas is on the brink of superstardom or not. He loves what he does regardless of whether he finds fame and fortune. Still, there's no doubt he'll keep showing up in lots more starring roles— and adorably awkward interviews too!

Nick's childhood hero was boxing champ Muhammad Ali, shown here in 1962.

CHAPTER ONE

A "NORMAL" KID

At the age of eleven, Nick already loved acting. He was a hit in his first major role in *About a Boy*.

When he's home in England, Nicholas Hoult sleeps under a poster of Muhammad Ali. It has a quote from the famous boxer: "I'm free to be what I want." That's so true for Nick! He's been a blue beast, a fairytale hero, a desert warrior, and a lovesick zombie, to name a few roles. When he was little, Nick wanted to grow up and become a dolphin. For this shape-shifting actor, the fun began long ago.

NICK BASICS

- HOBBIES: surfing, riding his motorcycle
- BEST ADVICE HE'S EVER GOTTEN: keep family close
- GUILTY PLEASURE: reading his sisters' magazines
- TRAIT HE DISLIKES MOST ABOUT HIMSELF: overthinking stuff
- REGRET: not paying better attention in school
- BAD HABIT: eating food straight from the carton
- BIGGEST FEAR: dying young

Some of Nick's family members join him at the 2013 premiere of *Jack the Giant Slayer* in Hollywood.

A Big, Happy Family

On December 7, 1989, Nicholas Hoult was born into a big, loving family outside of London, England. Nicholas's mother, Glenis, was a piano teacher. His father, Roger, was an airplane pilot. Both have since retired. To this day, Nick considers both of his parents his personal heroes.

Nicholas is the third of four children. His brother, James, was twelve and already into acting when Nicholas came along. Both of Nick's sisters, Rosie and Clarista, would also take to the stage. The Hoult kids have theater in their blood. Their great aunt Anna Neagle was a huge British star of the 1930s.

Still, Nicholas says his childhood was "very normal." He remembers running around his yard a lot. He made tree houses. He pretended to fight beasts and wrestle monsters.

The Hoults never let any family member think too much of him or herself. There are just too many people in their house who need attention—and too many people who don't want to deal with drama. This down-to-earth attitude just might explain Nick's humorous downplaying of his many talents.

Nick's mom (LEFT) helped him and all his siblings chase their acting dreams.

Getting Lucky

Nicholas says he **"just kind of ended up acting."** Then he **"got very lucky."** His sibs were actually more into it than he was. His parents weren't pushy, either. But when an opportunity came along, they helped him grab it.

When Nicholas was three, he went to see his big brother in a play.

11

Little Nick was totally mesmerized. The director couldn't get over it. The tot had the makings of a true actor, he said. He cast Nick in a famous play called *The Caucasian Chalk Circle*. Nick barely remembers anything about that first acting job.

A few years later, Nick was tagging along when his big sis Rosie went to see an agent. The agent agreed to work with Rosie—and she asked to work with Nicholas too! His parents gave their okay. When he was five, his agent sent him on his first audition. "Lucky" Nick got the part. He was psyched about his role in the dramatic comedy. All he had to do was sit under a table and shove cake in his mouth!

GIRL POWER

When Nick was nine, his brother, James, moved out of the house. Since Nick's dad was a pilot, he was gone a lot too. On most days, Nick was the only guy at home with his mom and two sisters. To this day, Nicholas feels comfortable around women.

Nicholas likes to hang out with his mom and older sister, Rosie.

Nicholas got his big break while acting with Toni Collette (CENTER) and Hugh Grant (RIGHT) in *About a Boy*

His Big Break

After that, the parts just kept coming. By the age of nine, Nick was a pro at doing TV work. His mother drove him to all his auditions. She always stayed with him on set.

When Nicholas was eleven, he got his first big break. He landed a leading role in a major movie. Nick had to get a goofy bowl cut to play Marcus in *About a Boy*. People made fun of his pointy eyebrows too. But he didn't mind. And later, he was over the moon when the film was nominated for an Oscar!

NOMINATED =
in the running for
an award

CHAPTER TWO

ACTING FOR REAL

As much as he loves it, Nick doesn't let acting define who he is.

After *About a Boy*, Nicholas stopped working so much. He still thought of acting as just a hobby. It was something fun he did outside of school.

Looking back, he's glad he took some time to get in touch with his "real" life. When he can, he still tries to take breaks between movies. **"It's important to have real-life experiences,"** he says. That helps him connect better with his characters.

A STUNT GONE WRONG!

When he was thirteen, Nicholas was doing a quick job for a TV show. He was tied to a chair and dangling from a bridge. A bus was supposed to stop inches away— except it didn't. As his mother looked on in horror, Nicholas's leg smashed through the bus's window. Luckily, Nick was okay.

Besides, Nicholas started having a huge growth spurt. By the age of fourteen, he was 6 feet (1.8 meters) tall! Eventually, he topped off at 6 feet 3 inches (1.9 m). Directors weren't exactly interested in a kid who was taller than the leading man.

Teenage Life

In 2004, Nick's "hobby" started to pick up again. He went to South Africa to film *Wah-Wah*, a drama about a family going through a divorce. The next year, he was cast as the son in *The Weather Man*.

But all in all, Nick was cool with just being a regular teen. He played

People noticed Nick's acting chops when he starred in *Wah-Wah* as a teen.

forward on his town's
basketball team.
He sang for a band
that played tunes by
Arctic Monkeys, a British rock group. To top it all
off, he did a stint as an assistant DJ at kiddie parties.

A Huge Leap

In 2007, Nick got the main role on a new British TV
show. Everyone was buzzing about the teen drama, called
Skins. Nicholas's character, Tony Stonem, was cruel and
controlling. His peers worshipped him. That would be a
real acting challenge for Nick!

This job was full-time, though. It would mean quitting
school at seventeen. Did Nick want it that badly? He says
he had a **"mini nervous breakdown"** deciding what to
do. But in the end, he took a deep breath and said yes.
He was ready to be an actor for real.

Nick's costars on *Skins* were like his family. FROM LEFT: Joe
Dempsie, Dev Patel, Nicholas, Mike Bailey, Mitch Hewer, April
Pearson, Aimee-Ffion Edwards, Larissa Wilson, and Hannah Murray.

Moving On and Up

After two seasons, almost the whole cast of *Skins* was fired. New actors took their places. British shows are different from US shows that way. The directors had planned that all along to keep the series fresh.

Nicholas had that uneasy feeling he still gets after jobs wrap. He hated to say good-bye to the cast. He actually wondered if he would ever work again.

In 2009, Nick got a phone call late one night. It was about an indie movie called *A Single Man*. One of the actors had dropped out at the last minute. Would Nicholas try out for the part? Days later, Nick was filming in California.

Nicholas sharpened his acting skills in the indie drama *A Single Man*.

INDIE MOVIE =
an independent movie, or a movie that is not made by a big-time Hollywood studio

Nicholas attends the 2011 Venice Film Festival with his *A Single Man* costars.

He played Kenny, a gay college student who saves his professor from committing suicide.

As *A Single Man* racked up awards, Nicholas earned a new respect from movie buffs. Was this sophisticated actor really the same geeky kid from *About a Boy*? Nicholas was showing his amazing powers to transform. And he had only just begun.

CRINGE!

Nicholas hates watching himself on-screen. Sometimes, he actually has to close his eyes. It's not just seeing his face blown up to fifty times its normal size. It's that he'll think, "Oh, I could have done that better!" Then he'll get an idea for something he wished he'd tried. Next time, Nick!

CHAPTER THREE

HELLO, HOLLYWOOD!

Nicholas challenges himself acting as supersmart student Hank McCoy (RIGHT) and his mutant counterpart, Beast (ABOVE), in *X-Men: First Class.*

Nick was in Australia when an urgent phone call woke him up in the middle of the night. His agent told him to hop on the next plane to London. Nicholas had landed an audition for *X-Men: First Class*. He had a shot to play scientist Hank McCoy, who morphs into the ferociously blue Beast.

Nicholas was sure he bombed the audition. But sure enough, he got the part! Nick felt like a giddy kid as he arrived on the set of *X-Men* in the summer of 2010. Beast was one of his favorite comic book characters of all time.

This role presented some unique challenges. For one, he was playing a younger version of a well-known character. Kelsey Grammer had played Hank in an earlier *X-Men* movie.

NICK'S IFS

- If he weren't an actor, he'd be a Formula One driver.
- If he could go on any vacation, he'd go to Brazil, during the World Cup.
- If he had one superpower, he'd pick teleporting.
- If he could go back in time, he'd visit the age of dinosaurs.
- If he could play any character, he'd be James Bond.

Nicholas actually really likes doing an American accent—which he'd have to do for X-Men. But this time, he had to nail the accent of just one famous actor. He watched hours of Grammer in old TV shows to get it right.

A second challenge was his costume. That furry blue outfit was hot … and heavy. Nick had to bulk up just to wear it. (Fortunately, one arm came off so he could at least go to the bathroom by himself!) Nick also had to figure out how to show emotions through his mask.

Nicholas got to perform some awesome stunts as Beast.

Nick's third challenge was Jennifer Lawrence. As the movie began filming, he developed a crush on his beautiful costar. The crush was mutual, and soon the two started dating. Suddenly, he became one-half of Hollywood's latest "it" couple. That attention made Nicholas squirm.

All challenges aside, Nick threw himself into his part. He gave 100 percent to the role of Hank McCoy/Beast. And fans everywhere agree that Nicholas nailed it.

Fairytale Hero

On *X-Men*, Nicholas got used to being on a big-budget movie set. But in the spring of 2011, *Jack the Giant Slayer* took first-day jitters to a whole new level. For the first time ever, Nick was the leading man on set. He had beat out plenty of competitors too. Luckily, director Bryan Singer had worked with Nicholas during *X-Men*. He knew Nick had a vulnerable side that was perfect for the role of Jack.

Nicholas and Jennifer didn't put their feelings toward each other on display when they first became a couple.

Jack the Giant Slayer used a ton of computer animation. Half the time, Nicholas was acting in front of a green screen. Tennis balls marked where the animated characters would get filled in later. Their voices came over a loudspeaker, so Nicholas knew when to say his lines.

At first, Nick was nervous about this career-changing job. But soon, he was too tired to be nervous. This was a big action flick. Nick really had to climb a fake beanstalk (made partly from celery). He learned to ride horses too. But in the end, the director put him on a barrel instead of on a horse. The director didn't want him to get hurt on the set. Later, animators used special effects to add a horse to those scenes. Nick, for his part, loved "riding" on the barrel! He couldn't believe he was getting paid to play like a kid.

ANIMATION = lifelike characters created by artists for TV or film

Nicholas enjoys playing in action movies like *Jack* and *X-Men*.

The brains in *Warm Bodies* were a sweet, cakey mixture. The only problem was that they got mixed up with dummy hair during Nick's big brain-eating scene. What could he do? He didn't want to force everyone to set up the whole scene again. He gave himself a pep talk. "I was like, just do it, do it!" And then he snarfed up those cake brains, wig hair and all!

Zombie Heartthrob

Nicholas had to bring that energy waaaaaaay down for his role in *Warm Bodies*. He was psyched to play R, the world's first-ever zombie heartthrob. Nick worked with a pro to get his movements right for R. This was a comedy, no doubt. But it had a serious message about the human need to connect. Nick didn't want that part lost in too much silliness.

At first, Nicholas did what he does with every role. He just experimented. He practiced his "zombie run" at the gym. That got some looks, for sure. In the end, the trick was to make his body feel really heavy. He also decided he wouldn't blink. His eyes burned like crazy. On the upside, Nick is now a total champ at staring contests!

Nicholas admits that he sometimes obsesses about stuff. Like, um … knitting. Nick had some time on his hands while filming *Mad Max*. So he taught himself to knit. He knitted 24–7 until he got sick of it. Then he dropped it just like that.

Nicholas poses with his sister at the L.A. premiere of *Warm Bodies*.

Good-byes and New Beginnings

In 2012, Nicholas headed to Namibia to film *Mad Max: Fury Road*. He will play the warrior Nux in that blockbuster, slated for 2014. Nick was in Africa's deserts for seven long months. During that time, he and Jennifer grew apart. In January 2013, the "it" couple decided to call things off for a while.

Nick and Jen stayed close friends, though—and that was a good thing, because that May they met up on the set of *X-Men: Days of Future Past*. Things could've been super awkward if the split hadn't been so friendly!

During filming, the two appeared to be getting along extremely well. By the end of the summer, it appeared that they may have even rekindled their romance.

In 2014 and beyond, expect to see Nicholas star in *Young Ones*, a sci-fi thriller. He'll also play an officer in *Birdsong*, set in World War II (1939–1945). Then he joins the cast of the mystery *Dark Places*.

As Nicholas's career keeps on getting bigger, he has no plans whatsoever to slow down. Yet he also notes that you never know what life may have in store. **"I'm just trying to go with the flow, see what happens, and hope for the best,"** he states. You can't argue with that grand plan. So far, it's worked out kind of great for the talented Nicholas Hoult!

ASK NICHOLAS

- ON STAYING SANE: "I like to keep busy. Otherwise my brain starts ticking and I will go mad."
- ON ACTING: "What I like about this job is that you never peak. There are always new challenges."
- ON FAME: "I enjoy the acting part, but then I forget that people are actually going to watch it."

NICHOLAS PICS!

Nicholas and costar Teresa Palmer laugh during a Warm Bodies promo event in Toronto, Canada.

Nick was all bow ties and smoldering looks with Matthew Goode (CENTER) and Colin Firth (LEFT) at the Venice premiere of A Single Man.

Nicholas attends a Jack press junket in the United Kingdom with costar Eleanor Tomlinson.

SOURCE NOTES

5.   Lesley Messer, "Nicholas Hoult Dated Jennifer Lawrence—but Insists He's No Heartthrob," *People*, February 28, 2013, http://www.people.com/people /article/0,,20677977,00.html.

5.   Van McNeil, "Warm Bodies Nicholas Hoult Interview" (blog), 99.1 the Mix podcast, January 30, 2013, http://www.991themix.com/Warm-Bodies-Nicholas-Hoult-Interview -/11315408?pid=293350.

5.   Marlow Stern, "Nicholas Hoult on 'Warm Bodies,' 'X-Men,' Jennifer Lawrence & More," *Daily Beast*, February 1, 2013, http://www.thedailybeast.com/articles/2013/02/01 /nicholas-hoult-on-warm-bodies-x-men-jennifer-lawrence-more.html.

6.   Niki Cruz, "The Staggering Nicholas Hoult," *Interview*, accessed May 22, 2013, http://www.interviewmagazine.com/film/nicholas-hoult-warm-bodies#.

6.   Sharon Knolle, "Nicholas Hoult: 20 Reasons We Love 'Warm Bodies' Star," *moviephone*, February 1, 2013, http://news.moviefone.com/2013/02/01/nicholas-hoult-reasons-we- love-warm-bodies_n_2597989.html.

7.   "Interview with Nicholas Hoult," *Vue*, accessed May 22, 2013, http://www.myvue.com /film-news/article/title/interview-with-nicholas-hoult.

9.   Ziba Adel, "Nicholas Hoult: 'Can You Not Just Say I Was Lighthearted and Witty?,'" *Guardian* (London), May 20, 2011, http://www.guardian.co.uk/film/2011/may/21 /nicholas-hoult-interview.

11.   Richard Godwin, "Hello Hollywood: Nicholas Hoult, the Boy from Berkshire, Becomes a Big Screen Superhero," *London Evening Standard*, March 8, 2013, http://www.standard .co.uk/lifestyle/esmagazine/hello-hollywood-nicholas-hoult-the-boy-from-berkshire -becomes-a-big-screen-superhero-8524292.html.

11.   "Your Questions," Facebook video, 3:53, posted by Nicholas Hoult, February 26, 2013, https://www.facebook.com/photo.php?v=10102726361386845.

15.   Stern, "Nicholas Hoult on 'Warm Bodies,' 'X-Men,' Jennifer Lawrence."

17.   Alice Fisher, "Hoult…Who Goes There?," *Guardian* (London), January 30, 2010, http://www.guardian.co.uk/film/2010/jan/31/nicholas-hoult-skins-bafta-hollywood.

19.   "Interview with Nicholas Hoult," *Vue*.

25.   "Nicholas Hoult Photo Shoot—JustJared.com Exclusive!," *Just Jared*, January 31, 2013, http://www.j-14.com/2013/01/j-14-exclusive-interview-nicholas-hoult-talks-warm -bodies-dating-love.html.

27.   Christopher Rosen, "Nicholas Hoult, 'Warm Bodies' Star, Remembers 'About a Boy,' Looks Forward to More 'X-Men,'" *Huffington Post*, January 29, 2013, http://www .huffingtonpost.com/2013/01/29/nicholas-hoult-warm-bodies_n_2575592.html.

27.   Shahesta Shaitly, "Nicholas Hoult: 'The Paparazzi Don't Care About Me,'" *Guardian* (London), January 26, 2013, http://www.guardian.co.uk/culture/2013/jan/26 /nicholas-hoult-paparazzi-warm-bodies.

27.   "Nicholas Hoult: I Wanted to Be a Dolphin," *Just Jared*, January 20, 2010, http://www .justjared.com/2010/01/20/nicholas-hoult-i-wanted-to-be-a-dolphin/.

27.   Ben Barna, "Rising Star Nicholas Hoult Flexes His Muscles in 'X-Men: First Class,'" *BlackBook*, June 3, 2011, http://www.blackbookmag.com/movies/rising-star-nicholas -hoult-flexes-his-muscles-in-x-men-first-class-1.23810.

MORE NICHOLAS INFO

Claremont, Chris, and John Byrne. *X-Men: Days of Future Past*. New York: Marvel Comics, 2011. Read the book before the blockbuster hits screens in summer 2014.

Higgins, Nadia. *Jennifer Lawrence: The Hunger Games' Girl on Fire*. Minneapolis: Lerner Publications, 2013. Get the inside scoop on Nick's Oscar-winning ex and X-Men costar.

Just Jared Jr.: Nicholas Hoult
http://www.justjaredjr.com/?s=nicholas+hoult
Get the latest news and photos of Nick—without the rumors. This fun site is organized from newest to oldest posts, so you can scroll down and see what Nick's been up to.

Nicholas's Facebook Page
https://www.facebook.com/NicholasHoult
This is the closest Nick gets to an official site. Unlike other stars, he doesn't link to everything that's out there. Nick reposts only the best videos and articles from the web.

Nicholas's Twitter Page
https://twitter.com/NicholasHoult
Nick joined Twitter in January 2013 to stop someone who was posing as him. Every so often, he'll tweet answers to fans' questions.

INDEX

The images in this book are used with the permission of: © Alberto E. Rodriguez/Getty Images, pp. 2, 5; © KMazur/WireImage/Getty Images, pp. 3 (top), 8 (top right); © Simon James /WireImage/Getty Images, pp. 3 (bottom), 14 (bottom); Donatella Giagnori/EIDON/Photoshot /Newscom, p. 4 (top left); Byron Purvis/AdMedia/Newscom, p. 4 (top right); MARIO ANZUONI /REUTERS/Newscom, p. 4 (bottom); © Helga Esteb/Shutterstock.com, p. 6; AP Photo/Arthur Mola /Invision, p. 7; © The Ring Magazine/Getty Images, p. 8 (top left); © Globe Photos/ZUMAPRESS. com, pp. 8 (bottom), 13; © Paul Smith/Featureflash/Shutterstock.com , p. 9; © s_bukley /Shutterstock.com, p. 10; © Dave Hogan/Getty Images, p. 11; © Dave Benett/Getty Images, p. 12; © Ferdaus Shamim/WireImage/Getty Images, p. 14 (top); Alex Jackson/WENN/Newscom, p. 15; © Samuel Goldwyn Films/Courtesy Everett Collection, p. 16; © Channel 4/Company Pictures /Courtesy Everett Collection, p. 17; © Weinstein Company/Courtesy Everett Collection, p. 18; Splash News/Newscom, p. 19; Murray Close/TM and Copyright © 20th Century Fox Film Corp. All rights reserved./Courtesy Everett Collection, p. 20 (bottom right); TM and Copyright © 20th Century Fox Film Corp. All rights reserved/Courtesy Everett Collection, p. 20 (top right); © Murray Close/Moviepix/Getty Images, pp. 20 (left), 22; AP Photo/Brian J. Ritchie/Hotsauce/Rex, p. 21; infuklo-105/INFphoto.com/Newscom, p. 23; © Warner Bros. Pictures/Courtesy Everett Collection, p. 24; © SUMMIT ENTERTAINMENT/SuperStock, p. 25; © StarMaxWorldwide/ImageCollect, p. 26; © Globe Photos/ImageCollect, p. 27; © Byron Purvis/AdMedia/ImageCollect, p. 28 (top left); © O'Neill/White/INFphoto.com/Newscom, p. 28 (bottom left); © Russ Elliot/AdMedia/ ImageCollect, p. 28 (right); © Graham Whitby/Globe Photos/ImageCollect, p. 29 (top); Kathy Hutchins/Hutchins Photo/Newscom, p. 29 (bottom left).

Front cover: © Byron Purvis/AdMedia/ImageCollect (main); © Steve Vas/Featureflash/Shutterstock. com (inset). Back cover: © Byron Purvis/AdMedia/ImageCollect.

Main body text set in Shannon Std Book 12/18.
Typeface provided by Monotype Typography.